Josie Goes On Holiday

Monica Hughes

Illustrated by Lisa Smith

RIGBY

Josie went on holiday with her dad.
Ravi and his dad went too.

On the first day, Josie's dad took Josie and Ravi on a long walk.

Josie's dad walked very fast.
"This is fun!" he said.

Josie and Ravi couldn't walk so fast.
"I'm tired!" said Josie.
"Wait for us!" said Ravi.

They got back to the tents.

"Did you have a good time?" asked Ravi's dad.

"We did, but we're very tired,"
said Josie and Ravi.
Then they fell asleep.

The next day, Ravi's dad
took Josie and Ravi canoeing.
"This is fun!" said Ravi's dad.

The canoe went very fast.
"I'm getting wet!" said Josie.
"Do we have to go so fast?" asked Ravi.

They got back to the tents.

"Did you have a good time?" asked Josie's dad.

"Yes, but we're very wet," said Josie and Ravi.

Then they fell asleep.

The next day, Josie and Ravi wanted to go horse-riding.

Josie and Ravi liked riding the horses.

"This is great fun!" said Josie.

"Come on!" said Ravi.

Josie's dad didn't like his horse.
He couldn't get it to go.
Ravi's dad didn't like his horse.
He couldn't get it to go.
"Wait for us!" they said.

When they got back to the tents,
Josie and Ravi weren't tired.
"I love horse-riding!" said Josie.
"So do I!" said Ravi.
"Can we do it again tomorrow?"

"We're too tired!" said the two dads.